30 Days of I Am

Debbie Z Almstedt

30 Days of I Am

Remembering Your Magnificence
Through
Zibu Angelic Symbols®

Debbie Z Almstedt

Debbie Z Almstedt

Copyright © 2019 by Debbie Zylstra Almstedt

All rights reserved. This book or any portion thereof may not be reproduced or used in any manner whatsoever without the express written permission of the publisher except for the use of brief quotations in a book review.

Printed in the United States of America

ISBN 978-0-9798302-9-7

First Printing, 2019

Text and artwork by
Debbie Zylstra Almstedt
ZibuAngelicSymbols.com

Cover Design by Sue Broome
SueBroome.com

DEDICATION

This book is dedicated to my daughter Alexandra, who is an angel here on earth. She has assisted me in awakening to my true purpose in being here and enriches my life daily with her love, joy, and insights.

Debbie Z Almstedt

30 Days of I Am

CONTENTS

INTRODUCTION 1
   How to Use This Book 2
   Drawing the Symbols 3
   Sensing the Energy of the Symbols 3
30 DAYS OF I AM 7
      Authenticity 8
      Balance 12
      Beauty 16
      Centeredness 20
      Creativity 24
      Faith 28
      Forgiveness 32
      Friendship 36
      Gratitude 40
      Harmony 44
      Honesty 48
      Hope 52
      Joy 56
      Kindness 60
      Light Heartedness 64
      Moderation 68
      Optimum Health 72
      Patience 76
      Persistence 80
      Resilience 84
      Self-Care 88
      Serenity 92
      Soul Reintegration 96

Truth	100
Unconditional Love	104
Unity	108
Unlimited Abundance	112
Vitality	116
Wisdom	120
World Peace	124
ABOUT THE AUTHOR	129

30 Days of I Am

INTRODUCTION

Do you remember who you are?

The Angels offer guidance in remembering and reclaiming your magnificence. These empowering affirmations were channeled from the Angels during my morning meditations.

The Angels are always whispering reminders to us of our greatness and our ability to create the lives we desire. Take a moment of quietude to look at what may appear to be blocks in your life. They could be outdated beliefs about yourself and your abilities or worthiness. Perhaps they are incorrect assumptions about your limitations. They are but illusions placed there by yourself, and you have the power to remove them.

The Angels invite you to step outside of yourself to release any and all perceived obstacles. Now is the time to embrace fully who you are and claim your power. Create your life as you desire.

You are the writer of your life story. You star in it and are meant to shine brightly. You have the power to create the stage, call in the other actors, determine the story line and the outcome.

In 2002, when I began channeling Zibu symbols, I heard the Angels repeatedly whisper, "Help them to remember—help them to remember." I was initially puzzled as I didn't understand what they were referring to and what there was to remember.

Clarity has come with time.

We are being invited to remember our magnificence, our gifts, our power, our beauty, our love and our passion for living! We are phenomenal creatures with incredible power to manifest what we desire when we remember these strengths.

Zibu symbols from the Angels have become a regular part of each day for me. The symbols act as a fascinating and easy way to see energy and sense it. They are keys to connect quickly with high vibrational energy intended to assist you in remembering who you are—your divine self that sometimes gets buried under debris from lower vibrational thoughts and experiences.

The Angels bring these fluid symbols as physical representation of high vibrational multi-dimensional energy.

At those times when you feel disconnected and doubt your abilities or question your physical or emotional strength, know that Zibu symbols offer a method to instantaneously realign with your true essence—that of pure unlimited energy from Spirit.

How to Use This Book

The affirmations place you in touch with the power of "I Am" statements as you remind yourself of who you are.

Thirty days of affirmations are featured which you can read as you begin each day for 30 consecutive days. You can read them sequentially or you can skip to the ones that seem to pull your attention. I invite you to spend time with an affirmation each day and check in at the end of 30 days to see how your energy has elevated to a more positive space.

Give thought to the words as you read them and then say them out loud. As you speak the words, listen to yourself. Taste the sweetness of the words as you express them. Feel the vibration of the words throughout your body.

Each time you speak the affirmations, your energy shifts. It raises up higher. Your heart expands and your light shines brighter.

An embellished Zibu symbol accompanies each affirmation along with guidance on the most optimal way to draw them. Drawing the symbols with your fingertips in the air or with pen on paper allows you to connect with the Angelic energy on a cellular level.

Angelic quotes appear throughout this book which came from Zephyrine, the Angel I work most closely with. They are offered as further inspiration.

Drawing the Symbols

Space is provided to practice drawing the symbols but also to capture any impressions or guidance from the Angelic Realm as you show up each day. The repetition of drawing will further assist you in connecting with the essence of each symbol.

Pay attention to the rhythm, speed, fluidity and how you are further guided by the Angels. Imagine the Angels holding your hand and guiding your pen effortlessly until the pattern becomes second nature.

The rhythm may rise and quicken, then slow down as the spiral is drawn. The three dots are drawn last as punctuation and emphasis.

A mantra is offered with each symbol. You are invited to speak the mantra as you draw. Feel the sensations in your heart and your body as you further connect with the Angelic vibration.

Sensing the Energy of the Symbols

You are encouraged to use all your senses to align yourself with this exquisite Angelic energy. Each person's experience is unique, so give yourself permission to relax and enjoy it.

Touch

Use your fingertips or pen to trace the symbols. Be fully present to pay close attention to the movement and rhythm. Allow your body to relax knowing that the beautiful energy is being absorbed on a cellular level and will remain with you.

Listen

Take several deep breaths to calm your mind and focus on hearing the energy. At times I can hear what sounds like a dry bristle brush on a rough canvas as it goes through the motion of tracing the symbols. At other times, I hear the ascending and descending glissando of a slide-whistle which matches the rise and fall of the pen stroke. Remember to stay quiet to hear any guidance that is whispered to you. The Angels have your attention and are eager to bring inspiration with words of love and encouragement.

Smell

Remember to breathe deeply as you invite the energy into your physical body. Imagine it blending into every part of your being. I often smell the sweetness of roses while savoring the energy. Again, each person's experience will be unique. Release any preconceived expectations and allow your encounter to be revealed.

Taste

A client recently expressed her surprise that she could actually taste the energy while holding a Zibu piece I had created specifically for her. Experiment and be open to what the Angels desire to bring you. Relax knowing there is no right or wrong way. You will be gently guided.

See

Behold the graceful symbols. Gaze at them. Visually, they represent gentle yet powerful energy. Open this book to a random page or choose a specific symbol to spend time with. Enjoy gazing at a chosen symbol or combination of symbols. They can effortlessly shift the energy of your surroundings in a positive manner. This is most apparent when you are clearly in the present moment and aware.

Everyone has certain senses that are stronger than others or a preferred way of sensing their surroundings. Know that the same is true while you interact with the Zibu symbols. Pay attention to which sense is strongest for you and put your attention there.

This book focuses on 30 Zibu symbols; however, there are many more. I published the book "Zibu: The Power of Angelic Symbology" in 2007 as a concise resource guide of 88 symbols with channeled messages for each one.

Another resource available to you is the Zibu Affirmation and Oracle Deck, which features the same 88 symbols with one-line affirmations. Many people find it easier to work with the symbols on tarot-sized cards. It offers the option of pulling a card a day to focus attention upon it. The deck can also be used for intuitive readings for yourself or others. Having the symbols on individual cards allows you to place the cards where you can see them throughout the day or place them in a space where you desire to shift the energy, such as the "harmony" symbol in a family room or office.

My intention is to provide guided inspiration using Zibu Angelic Symbols. These are options for you to use. Please remember that this is not a project but rather an invitation. Make it your own experience. Have fun and enjoy!

Debbie Z Almstedt

30 Days of I Am

30 DAYS OF I AM

Debbie Z Almstedt

Debbie Z Almstedt, Zibu Angelic Symbols®

30 Days of I Am

Authenticity

"I am Authenticity, and I shine brightest when I am true to myself. My interactions with others are genuine as I express my authentic self. I celebrate my unique spirit. I thrive knowing I compromise myself for no one. I value who I am and the gifts I bring to the world. And so it is."

Mantra: Asi (ah'-see)

- ♥ Focus your attention on the Angelic symbol for authenticity.
- ♥ Remember the importance of standing strong in who you are.
- ♥ Trace this symbol from the top left spiral through the complete symbol in one movement finishing in the bottom right spiral.
- ♥ Feel the twists and turns as you connect with this distinctive energy.
- ♥ Speak the mantra several times and listen to the vibration.
- ♥ All of this is to support you in being true to yourself.

Debbie Z Almstedt

*"Zibu symbols
open up energetic portals
for Heavenly transformation."*

~ Angel Zephyrine

30 Days of I Am

Authenticity

Debbie Z Almstedt, Zibu Angelic Symbols®

30 Days of I Am

Balance

"I am Balance. I stop and take a cleansing breath and see the balance within. Balance gives me strength and keeps me in an enjoyable space between two extremes. I recognize that I am balance and can tap into that energy at any time. I have it available to me when I need it as it is always with me, as me. As I envision that I am balance, I see that in others as well. I am balance, just as we are balance. And so it is."

Mantra: Himu (hee'-moo)

- ♥ Hold your palm over the Zibu symbol for balance.

- ♥ Envision the Angelic energy radiating from the symbol to your hand.

- ♥ Speak the mantra to savor the sound.

- ♥ Draw the fluid shape with ease from left to right and feel the rhythm. It starts with a spiral and ends with a spiral.

- ♥ Breathe in the beautiful energy of balance knowing that it resides within.

Debbie Z Almstedt

"Your Angels await your invitation to assist and offer loving guidance."

~ Angel Zephyrine

30 Days of I Am

Balance

Debbie Z Almstedt

Debbie Z Almstedt, Zibu Angelic Symbols®

30 Days of I Am

Beauty

"I am Beauty. I express beauty by the words I speak and the actions I take. I share this beauty with those around me and beyond directly from my heart, as that is what I embody. I am beauty on the inside and out. I know this to be true. I am beauty, and beauty is me. And so it is."

Mantra: Arani (ah-rah'-nee)

- ♥ Say the mantra as you gaze at this Zibu symbol.
- ♥ Feel the energetic vibration in your heart.
- ♥ Know that you embody this always.
- ♥ Take a deep breath as you draw the symbol left to right and top to bottom.
- ♥ Exhale as you celebrate this truth.
- ♥ Feel the energy, see it in your mind's eye, and allow it to radiate out to others.

*"Beauty is
Spirit expressing itself
in human form."*

~ Angel Zephyrine

30 Days of I Am

Beauty

Debbie Z Almstedt

Debbie Z Almstedt, Zibu Angelic Symbols®

Centeredness

"I am Centeredness. As I take a deep breath, I feel all aspects of myself coming into alignment. From this place of centeredness, I am rebalanced as I prepare to move forward in confidence. I am grounded and enjoy sure-footedness with each step. Centeredness is who I am. And so it is."

Mantra: Akunata (ah-koo-nah'-tah)

- ♥ Feel the fluid movement of the energy of this Zibu symbol.

- ♥ Start by drawing the symbol from the bottom left spiral up to the top and then gently flowing down to the bottom right spiral.

- ♥ Envision this symbol within your energetic body from your feet up to your head and returning to the feet.

- ♥ Repeat the mantra slowly several times.

- ♥ Breathe deeply knowing that you receive additional support as you claim who you are.

"Centeredness will allow one to leap forward with sure-footedness and security and steadiness."

~ Angel Zephyrine

Centeredness

I I I I I

Debbie Z Almstedt

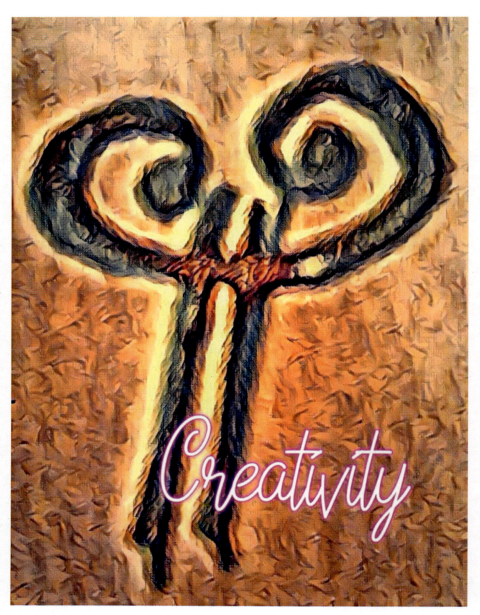

Debbie Z Almstedt, Zibu Angelic Symbols®

Creativity

"I am Creativity. Creativity resides within me and as me. I can bring it to the surface as I desire. I have the capacity to express creativity in whatever situation I choose, including discovering a creative solution to any challenge before me. Creativity is always available to me as my exclusive expression. I create beauty from this precious gift within. And so it is."

Mantra: Imono (ee-moh'-noh)

- ♥ Spend some time gazing at the Zibu symbol and sensing its energy.

- ♥ Trace the shape with your fingertips from the left spiral to the right spiral and complete the symbol with parallel lines from top to bottom.

- ♥ Feel the movement of the healing energies that swirl within this shape.

- ♥ Repeat the affirmation above and take three deep breaths as you envision bringing that energy into your lungs.

- ♥ How do you feel as you remember this aspect of yourself?

"As you embrace this symbol for creativity, know that you are a conduit for divine expression."

~ Angel Zephyrine

Creativity

Debbie Z Almstedt

Debbie Z Almstedt, Zibu Angelic Symbols®

Faith

"I am Faith. It is what I am. I have an unending belief in myself and in the positive outcome of all situations in which I am involved. I create these situations knowing I have what it takes to successfully navigate through them. I am faith, and I believe that all things are possible. And so it is."

Mantra: Anuba (ah-noo'-bah)

- ♥ Hold the palm of your hand over the Zibu symbol for Faith.

- ♥ Feel that strong connection to your Angels and remember who you are.

- ♥ Take a deep breath and fill your lungs with the energy of this powerful symbol.

- ♥ Whisper the mantra several times.

- ♥ Draw the symbol either in the air with your fingertips or on paper—top to bottom and left to right finishing with three dots moving from top to bottom—to punctuate the statement of energy and intention.

Debbie Z Almstedt

"Faith is an unending belief of the goodness and beauty in all experiences."

~ Angel Zephyrine

Faith

Ho Ho Ho Ho Ho

Debbie Z Almstedt

Debbie Z Almstedt, Zibu Angelic Symbols®

Forgiveness

"I am Forgiveness. It is my nature to release and let go of lower vibrational thoughts and grudges. I am forgiveness, and I can see the tremendous benefits of forgiving myself and others. As I am forgiveness, I lighten my heart and can move forward with grace. And so it is."

Mantra: Anka (ahn'-kah)

- ♥ To bring this sweet energy within and be reminded that you are indeed forgiveness, take a deep breath as you look at the colorful image of this Angelic symbol.

- ♥ Draw it in the air with your fingertips three times.

- ♥ As you do so, speak the mantra.

- ♥ Be aware of how the energy changes path and is redirected in a positive manner.

- ♥ Gently tap your heart chakra as a reminder that this energy resides within.

*"Forgiveness releases
and frees all of those involved."*

~ Angel Zephyrine

Forgiveness

I I I I I

Debbie Z Almstedt

Debbie Z Almstedt, Zibu Angelic Symbols®

Friendship

"I am Friendship. I demonstrate it daily. My open heart and extended arms allow me to express the energy of friendship. I invite others into this magnificent connection as we celebrate our God expression. I am a beautiful gift to others, as they are to me. And so it is."

Mantra: Tama (tah'-mah)

- ♥ Place both hands over this Zibu symbol.

- ♥ Feel the energy radiating up into your palms.

- ♥ As your cells awaken to this energy, take three gentle breaths and slowly exhale.

- ♥ Trace the symbol with your fingertips starting with the top spiral over and down.

- ♥ Finish the symbol with the second line going left to right ending in the second spiral.

- ♥ Take a deep breath and as you exhale, say the mantra.

- ♥ You now have connected with the Angelic energy on a cellular level.

*"The [Zibu] language
will help humans to
remember their divine role
on this earth plane."*

~ Angel Zephyrine

Friendship

Debbie Z Almstedt

Debbie Z Almstedt, Zibu Angelic Symbols®

Gratitude

"I am Gratitude, and I vibrate at the high frequency of grace. As such, I attract that which matches my frequency. I acknowledge the power to create my own reality. I am gratitude, and I attract all things positive. I place my attention on the blessings which surround me, knowing they are magnified exponentially. And so it is."

Mantra: Anu (ah'-noo)

- ♥ Inhale and feel this energy throughout your whole being.

- ♥ Draw this Angelic symbol in the air three times starting in the middle moving downwards and rising gracefully into the spiral.

- ♥ As you slowly draw this, repeat the mantra.

- ♥ It is a prayer with your voice and hands as you express that which you are.

Debbie Z Almstedt

"Gratitude is a blessed state to view the world, as it shifts the focus away from the negative and magnifies the positive."

~ Angel Zephyrine

30 Days of I Am

Gratitude

Debbie Z Almstedt

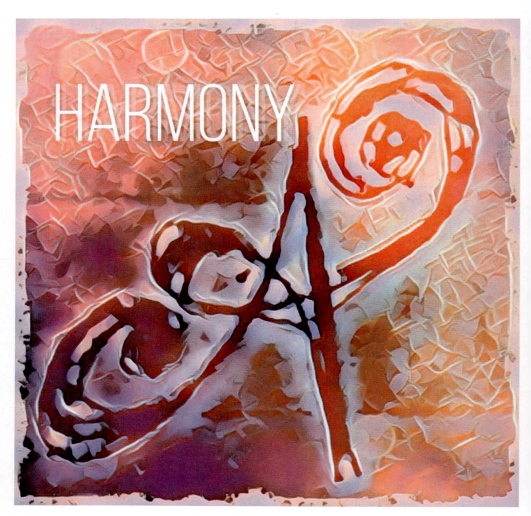

Debbie Z Almstedt, Zibu Angelic Symbols®

Harmony

"I am Harmony. I bring this positive energy to every situation and every encounter. This uplifting energy smooths the rough edges of any discord. I am the calming force that allows energy to flow effortlessly. I am harmony, and I am peace within and without. And so it is."

Mantra: Onoko (oh'-noh-koh)

- ♥ Draw the Angelic symbol from bottom left to top right, beginning with the spiral and ending with a spiral.

- ♥ Feel the stop and go rhythm of the energy.

- ♥ Hold this symbol to your heart and inhale knowing you embody this soothing energy.

- ♥ Say the mantra slowly savoring the exhalation of the sound.

- ♥ Feel the presence of the Angels and celebrate who you are.

Debbie Z Almstedt

"The harmony created by reconnecting with one another will have a tremendous impact on the world."

~ Angel Zephyrine

Harmony

Debbie Z Almstedt

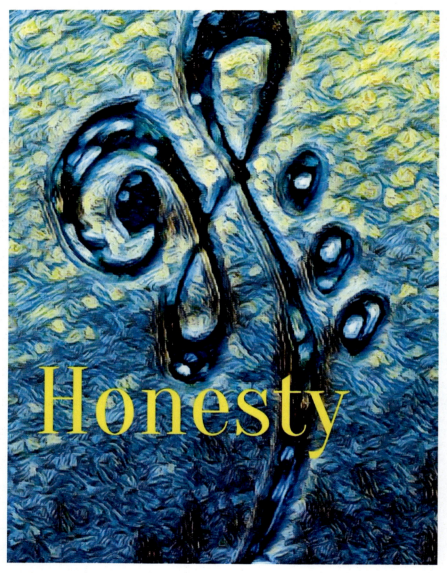

Debbie Z Almstedt, Zibu Angelic Symbols®

Honesty

"I am Honesty. Honesty is what I am. And being so, I am truthful with others as I express myself through kindness. More importantly, I am truthful with myself. I carry no illusions about who I am. I am honest with myself and accurately see who I am. I am honesty. And so it is."

Mantra: Kana (kah'-nah)

- ♥ The energy of this Angelic symbol is fluid just like all the others.

- ♥ Feel the movement and the rhythm as you draw the symbol.

- ♥ Speak the mantra several times.

- ♥ Pay close attention to how this high vibration feels to you.

- ♥ Let it echo throughout your body and mind.

- ♥ As you draw it, we invite you to take a gentle breath in and remember that you embody the energy that the symbol represents.

"Honesty begins with seeing the truth within."

~ Angel Zephyrine

30 Days of I Am

Honesty

𝓗 𝓗 𝓗 𝓗 𝓗 𝓗

Debbie Z Almstedt

Debbie Z Almstedt, Zibu Angelic Symbols®

30 Days of I Am

Hope

"I am Hope. I embody it, and I have an unending belief in the positive outcome of every situation before me. Hope is the life preserver which keeps me afloat during times of uncertainty. I trust and have faith, and I utilize hope as the lens through which I view my world. And so it is."

Mantra: Rizu (ree'-zoo)

- ♥ Take a slow gentle breath to bring in the energy of this Angelic healing symbol.

- ♥ Say the mantra as you exhale.

- ♥ Connect further by drawing the symbol on paper left to right and top to bottom punctuating the movement with three dots top to bottom.

- ♥ Sense the energy expanding throughout your body to remove any trace of doubt.

- ♥ Know that all is well in your world.

"Hope gives life meaning and connects you with something greater than yourself."

~ Angel Zephyrine

Hope

Debbie Z Almstedt

Debbie Z Almstedt, Zibu Angelic Symbols®

Joy

"I am Joy. It is the spark that resides within. Joy is the high vibrational energy I transmit. It activates a passion for living and provides motivation to savor every moment. It illuminates my day. I share this bright light of joy with those I meet knowing we all receive blessings in the process. And as I am, we are. And so it is."

Mantra: Anana (ah-nah'-nah)

- ♥ Draw the Zibu symbol slowly...top to bottom, left to right.
- ♥ Add the horizontal line left to right.
- ♥ Punctuate the symbol with three dots left to right.
- ♥ Slowly breathe the energy in.
- ♥ As you exhale, say the mantra.
- ♥ Allow the energy to expand within you.
- ♥ See the same joy within each person you meet or even think of today, as we are all one.

*"Zibu symbols
are keys to open
the locked memories."*

~ Angel Zephyrine

Debbie Z Almstedt

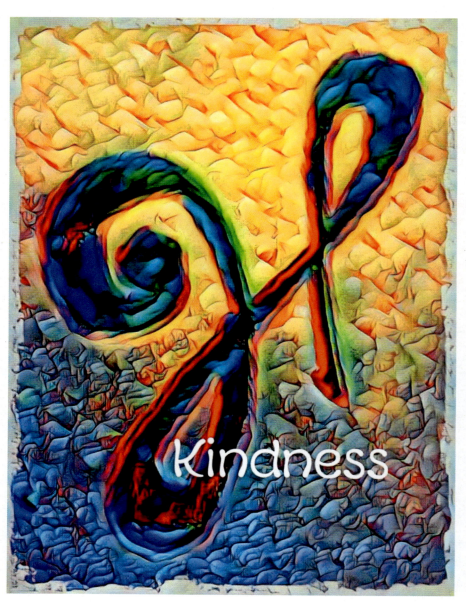

Debbie Z Almstedt, Zibu Angelic Symbols®

30 Days of I Am

Kindness

"I am Kindness, and my actions and words reflect that in every moment of every day. What I send out into the world begins in my heart and is spoken through kindness. I experience the sweetness of the expressed words knowing my life, as well as the lives of those around me, is enriched. And so it is."

Mantra: Hazu (hah'-zoo)

- ♥ Enjoy the graceful line of the Zibu symbol for kindness.

- ♥ Draw the symbol in the air with your fingertips to express this energy.

- ♥ Breathe it in and sense how smooth the energy feels as it washes over you.

- ♥ Gently trace the symbol top to bottom and left to right. Visualize it placed upon your throat chakra creating a filter through which your spoken words will pass.

- ♥ Envision the shift in energy of the gentle words you desire to speak knowing the positive difference they make.

- ♥ Thank your Angels for their assistance.

"Offer kindness freely
to those around you,
as all will reap great benefits."

~ Angel Zephyrine

30 Days of I Am

Kindness

Debbie Z Almstedt

Debbie Z Almstedt, Zibu Angelic Symbols®

30 Days of I Am

Light Heartedness

"I am Light Heartedness. I entertain uplifting thoughts infused with love and light. I release the burden of heaviness in lower vibrational thoughts and beliefs. I lighten my step and lighten my mood by looking to the light and the blessings in my life. As I embody this positive energy, it is easily transmitted to others and illuminates our paths. And so it is."

Mantra: Koha (koh'-hah)

- ♥ Stop for a moment and feel the high vibration of the Angelic symbol.

- ♥ Take a couple gentle breaths and settle into this energy.

- ♥ Draw the symbol in the air with your fingertips becoming aware of the fluid movement of the energy.

- ♥ As you do so, speak the mantra.

- ♥ Give thanks to the Angels for the beautiful reminder of who you are.

*"Remember to look to the light
and feel the lightness in your heart."*

~ Angel Zephyrine

Light Heartedness

H H H H H

Debbie Z Almstedt

Debbie Z Almstedt, Zibu Angelic Symbols®

Moderation

"I am Moderation. I navigate the gray area between the two extremes and do so with ease. I see the blessing of moderating my actions which brings with it a beautiful balance in my life. This balance allows a lovely flow of possibilities to open for me. Life is good. And so it is."

Mantra: Nona (noh'-nah)

- ♥ Enjoy the simplicity of this Angelic symbol.

- ♥ It is a smooth graceful movement from the top spiral down to the bottom spiral.

- ♥ Trace the symbol with your fingertips and repeat the mantra.

- ♥ Take a moment to embrace this energy knowing it provides a gentle reminder to enjoy the space between the extremes.

Debbie Z Almstedt

"Benefits can be received by either holding or beholding the Zibu symbols."

~ Angel Zephyrine

Moderation

Debbie Z Almstedt

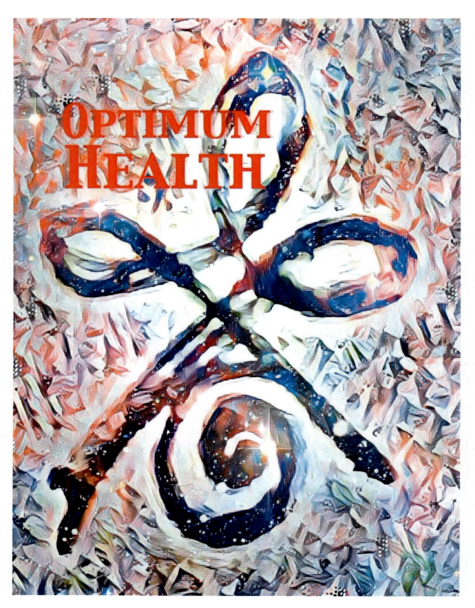

Debbie Z Almstedt, Zibu Angelic Symbols®

Optimum Health

"I am Optimum Health. As I claim this and know this as truth, all aspects of my body resonate with the energy of vibrant health. My body is a precious temple for my soul, and I see it as the healthy vessel it is. I accept this and celebrate it. And so it is."

Mantra: Hatumi (hah-too'-mee)

- ♥ Gaze into the depths of this symbolic image of healing energy.
- ♥ Take a moment to breathe this energy in allowing it to permeate all your cells.
- ♥ Use your fingertips to trace this image from bottom left up to three graceful loops and back down to the spiral.
- ♥ Speak the mantra as you trace the symbol again.
- ♥ Know that you have connected with this heavenly energy which is brought to you from the Angels.
- ♥ Express gratitude knowing that it is done.

*"Breathe life into your body
and envision it as the healthy temple
it is intended to be."*

~ Angel Zephyrine

Optimum Health

Debbie Z Almstedt

Debbie Z Almstedt, Zibu Angelic Symbols®

30 Days of I Am

Patience

"I am Patience. I enjoy each moment of every day of my life journey. I appreciate the magnificence of divine right timing. I take action when needed and allow things to unfold with grace and ease knowing it is perfection. I embody patience. And so it is."

Mantra: Anoko (ah-noh'-koh)

- ♥ Take a few breaths to settle into the present moment.

- ♥ Connect with the energy of this Angelic symbol by drawing it slowly left to right then down into the spiral.

- ♥ Punctuate this energy with three dots from left to right.

- ♥ Slowly repeat the mantra three times.

- ♥ Enjoy the energy of this symbol knowing that nothing needs to be rushed and all is unfolding beautifully.

*"Patience comes
from being
in the moment."*

~ Angel Zephyrine

Patience

Debbie Z Almstedt

Debbie Z Almstedt, Zibu Angelic Symbols®

Persistence

"I am Persistence as I continue forward even when faced with challenges. I see the value of continuing to show up each day and do my best. I know the benefit of continuing to take steps forward, even if just baby steps. I am persistence, and I keep going. It serves me well. And so it is."

Mantra: Atu (ah'-too)

- ♥ Spend some time looking at the shapes in the symbol.
- ♥ As you draw this symbol left to right, sense the energy in the loops which pull back to the left and catapults forward to the right.
- ♥ This has a powerful energy to it.
- ♥ Trace it again two more times and embrace the rhythm of the movement.
- ♥ As you do so, repeat the mantra.
- ♥ Breathe it in knowing that this is the energy you embody.

*"Zibu symbols
offer a direct energetic connection
with your Angels."*

~ Angel Zephyrine

Persistence

Debbie Z Almstedt

Debbie Z Almstedt, Zibu Angelic Symbols®

30 Days of I Am

Resilience

"I am Resilience. I hold on to hope and faith to assist me in bouncing back from any challenges I encounter. I know my strength will see me through. I am strong, and I am resilient. And so it is."

Mantra: Inoko (ee'-noh-koh)

- ♥ View the Angelic symbol and feel its strength.

- ♥ Breathe deeply as you draw the symbol from spiral to spiral, top to bottom. Then draw the parallel lines, and finish with the three dots for punctuation.

- ♥ It has a special rhythm that resonates throughout your body.

- ♥ Take it in and express gratitude as you repeat the mantra.

"The frequency level of the
[Zibu] language will remove the veils
which keep humans from
seeing clearly and remembering their roles."

~ Angel Zephyrine

Resilience

Debbie Z Almstedt

Debbie Z Almstedt, Zibu Angelic Symbols®

Self-Care

"I am Self-Care. I see the importance of cherishing and caring for myself first, so I may give of myself to others without depletion. I see my value, and I lovingly nurture myself. I acknowledge that there is nothing selfish about caring for my needs. I thrive beautifully because of this. And so it is."

Mantra: Kinota (kee-noh'-tah)

- Follow the energy of this Angelic symbol from spiral to spiral, left to right.

- Feel the nurturing sensation as you allow your fingertips to trace the image and absorb the energy.

- Repeat the mantra three times.

- Enjoy this energetic reminder to lovingly and compassionately care for yourself.

Debbie Z Almstedt

"Each soul is entrusted with a physical container. It is a sacred temple to be cared for with the utmost of reverence and love."

~ Angel Zephyrine

Self - Care

Debbie Z Almstedt

Debbie Z Almstedt, Zibu Angelic Symbols®

Serenity

"I am Serenity. It is within me. It is me, and I am it. I can bring that to the surface at any moment I choose. It is my choice to focus on the calm essence of serenity. As I do, I feel connected with all. I am serenity. We are serenity. And so it is."

Mantra: Adu (ah'-doo)

- ♥ Gaze upon the calm image of the Zibu symbol for serenity.
- ♥ Know that your Angels are with you.
- ♥ Draw the symbol slowly starting at the top. Follow the curves to the left and then the right. Finish into the spiral.
- ♥ Take a moment to truly feel that calm energy and take a gentle breath to remember the message.
- ♥ Speak the mantra to further connect with the energy.
- ♥ All is well.

"*Symbols act as visual cues
of what is happening
on a non-visible level.*"

~ Angel Zephyrine

Serenity

Debbie Z Almstedt

Debbie Z Almstedt, Zibu Angelic Symbols®

Soul Reintegration

"I am Soul Reintegration. I call back to me the parts of my soul which have fractured off during times of trauma. I lovingly welcome back those aspects of myself. I feel myself becoming whole once again, and I give thanks for this precious gift. And so it is."

Mantra: Ritan (ree-tan')

- ♥ Place your hands over this Zibu symbol to feel its full energy.
- ♥ Let your palms absorb the powerful healing energies.
- ♥ Visualize drawing the symbol from top to bottom and up again. Follow the zig zag down to the spiral.
- ♥ Repeat the mantra.
- ♥ Give thanks knowing it is done.

"Zibu symbols are Angelic energy which can ripple out to positively affect those in its path."

~ Angel Zephyrine

Soul Reintegration

Debbie Z Almstedt

Debbie Z Almstedt, Zibu Angelic Symbols®

Truth

"I am Truth. It is the only way I can be. I feel truth ripple up from my very core, and I express it in my words and my actions. I trust my internal guidance to verify what rings true for me. I value it, and it is unmistakable. And so it is."

Mantra: Hamani (hah-mah'-nee)

- ♥ The movement of energy in this Angelic symbol begins at the top spiral and flows down to the right and then left loop and finishes up in the spiral at the bottom.

- ♥ Draw this a few times in the air and savor the effortless fluidity.

- ♥ Breathe it into your solar plexus and let it reside there as a reminder of your ability to sense the "gut feeling" of what resonates as truth when you hear it or see it.

- ♥ As you exhale, say the mantra.

*"Take time to listen within
to hear the loving guidance
your Angels are whispering to you."*

~ Angel Zephyrine

Truth

Debbie Z Almstedt

Debbie Z Almstedt, Zibu Angelic Symbols®

Unconditional Love

"I am Unconditional Love. Love resides within me just as it resides within each person. Love is all there is really. Unconditional love is as divine love—pure without any expectations and no conditions need be met. It is who I am. It is loving as Spirit deems most holy. I embody that love. And so it is."

Mantra: Reko (ree-koh')

- Re-read the affirmation and let the words sink in as a reminder of what is true.

- Draw the graceful Angelic symbol from right spiral to left spiral—parallel lines left to right—then three dots top to bottom to accent the energy.

- Breathe in the energy to allow it to reach every portion of yourself.

- Speak the mantra as you exhale.

- Smile knowing it is so. It is so. It is so.

Debbie Z Almstedt

"Unconditional Love parallels Divine Love."

~ Angel Zephyrine

Unconditional Love

Debbie Z Almstedt

Debbie Z Almstedt, Zibu Angelic Symbols®

Unity

"I am Unity. I combine all aspects of myself to become whole and strong. I am unity as I connect with others in my community and the world. I celebrate that I am connected with all. There is no separation. All are one. And so it is."

Mantra: Tatano (tah'-tah-no)

- ♥ Breathe in the love associated with this Angelic symbol.

- ♥ Feel the energy expand through your body as you draw the symbol from the left spiral up to the top loop and back down again to the right spiral.

- ♥ As you do so, say the mantra each time you draw the symbol.

- ♥ This graceful symbol is like an embrace from your Angels.

- ♥ Smile and express gratitude to your Angels for this beautiful reminder of your true essence.

"Unity is a combining of all aspects of yourself."

~ Angel Zephyrine

30 Days of I Am

Unity

Debbie Z Almstedt

Debbie Z Almstedt, Zibu Angelic Symbols®

Unlimited Abundance

"I am Unlimited Abundance. It is who I am. There is no separation, as I am one with abundance. I easily express abundance in every thought, action and word. I take great delight as I observe this out-picturing of abundance in my life. And so it is."

Mantra: Lahika (lah-hee'-kah)

- ♥ To connect with the energy of this Angelic symbol, draw it on paper so you may hear the movement of the energy.

- ♥ It begins in the spiral and gently moves down to the bottom and continues to the right.

- ♥ It is punctuated by the three marks to the left from top to bottom.

- ♥ Speak the mantra as you draw the symbol.

- ♥ Pay close attention to the sound and physical sensation as you draw the symbol knowing that you take this in on a cellular level through this process.

Debbie Z Almstedt

*"When the pathways
are cleared of debris,
the natural flow of abundance
can run freely."*

~ Angel Zephyrine

30 Days of I Am

Unlimited Abundance

Debbie Z Almstedt

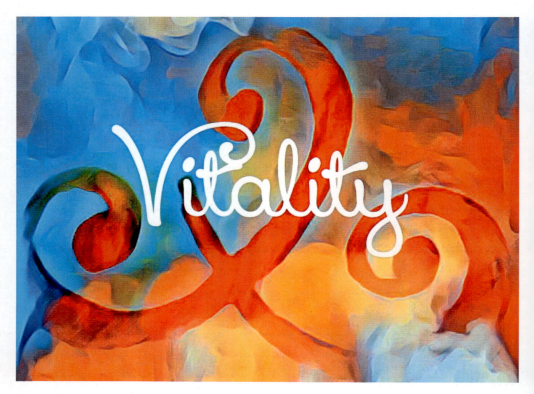

Debbie Z Almstedt, Zibu Angelic Symbols®

Vitality

"I am Vitality. I embody the true essence of divine energy. I am full of life force energy. Each day as I awaken, I feel the bright spark of vitality within me. It is my true nature. As I celebrate this within me, I celebrate for those around me as well, as we are all one. We are vitality. And so it is."

Mantra: Hamada (hah-mah'-dah)

- ♥ Spend some time gazing at this lovely visual representation of the energy of vitality.

- ♥ Draw it out either on paper or in the air—from top to bottom, left to right.

- ♥ Envision that energy of vitality in every cell of your body.

- ♥ Repeat the mantra as you do so.

- ♥ Take it in and express gratitude.

Debbie Z Almstedt

*"Zibu symbols
open up energetic portals
for Heavenly transformation."*

~ Angel Zephyrine

30 Days of I Am

Vitality

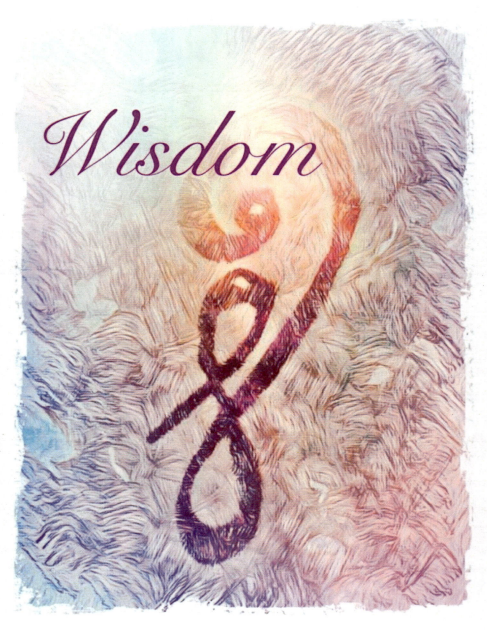

Debbie Z Almstedt, Zibu Angelic Symbols®

Wisdom

"I am Wisdom. I acknowledge the wisdom that resides within. I take time to quiet my mind to listen to the whisper of guidance. It is limitless. I relax into the knowing that wisdom is available to me when I choose, as I am this wisdom. It is me. And so it is."

Mantra: Azula (ah-zoo'-lah)

- ♥ Feel the fluidity of the Zibu symbol for wisdom.
- ♥ Follow the energy as you trace it up and back down and around, finishing up in the spiral.
- ♥ Sense the rhythm of this movement within your heart.
- ♥ Speak the mantra each time you trace the symbol.
- ♥ The connection is divine as the Angels bring you reminders of who you are.

"Slip into that space of knowing without any doubt whatsoever that all is available to you with grace and ease."

~ Angel Zephyrine

30 Days of I Am

Wisdom

Debbie Z Almstedt

Debbie Z Almstedt, Zibu Angelic Symbols®

World Peace

30 Days of I Am

"I am World Peace. I see how I contribute my inner peace to the community of the world. I take great delight in knowing my peaceful energy and thoughts make a positive difference to those around me and extend out further to the world. I cherish this as I remember that my peace makes a positive difference. And so it is."

Mantra: Amin (ah'-mihn)

- ♥ Stop for a moment and appreciate the contribution you make to the world with your peaceful thoughts and actions.

- ♥ Feel the energy of this Angelic symbol as it amplifies the peace within to radiate out into the world.

- ♥ Take a deep cleansing breath and exhale.

- ♥ Draw this symbol from top left through to bottom right—from spiral to spiral.

- ♥ Savor this energy as you breathe it in softly.

- ♥ Repeat the mantra as you do so.

*"The world can be a
safe and harmonious place
when you each contribute peace."*

~ Angel Zephyrine

30 Days of I Am

World Peace

Debbie Z Almstedt

ABOUT THE AUTHOR

Debbie Z Almstedt is an intuitive channel for the Angelic Realm, author, and artist. Her work with Angels spans over 15 years and is expressed in her original art, handcrafted jewelry, channel writings, and messages.

In 2002 Debbie began to receive the language of the Angels directly and channeled 88 unique symbols and messages. Known as *Zibu Angelic Symbols*, her drawings feature fluid and graceful designs intended to assist people in their daily lives. The 88 symbols are imbued with energies of hope, love, and encouragement directly from the Angelic Realm.

Debbie incorporates *Zibu Angelic Symbols* into her art, jewelry, and writing created in her art studio and sacred space located in Mesa, Arizona. She finds inspiration working with wire, metal and semi-precious gemstones, henna, pen and ink.

Visit ZibuAngelicSymbols.com for more information, or contact Debbie directly to book an individual reading at ZibuAngelicSymbols@gmail.com.

Made in the USA
Las Vegas, NV
05 March 2021